I am Hope:

The first poetic collection by Esperanza Habla

© 2014 La Luna Press

Previously copyrighted as:

<u>Between Yesterday</u>: The Creative Collective Poetic Works of Esperanza Habla Volume 1

<u>Just Me</u>: The Creative Collective Poetic Works of Esperanza Habla Volume 2

ISBN: 978-0-9915104-1-2

Library of Congress Control Number: 2014952426

Cover design and all photographs by Esperanza Habla
Author portrait courtesy of Kristen Pugh Photography
Logo for La Luna Press by Adam Whitaker

All rights reserved. No part of this publication may be reproduced, distributed, or transmitted in any form or by any means, including photocopying, recording, or other electronic or mechanical methods, without the prior written permission of the publisher, except in the case of brief quotations embodied in critical reviews and certain other noncommercial uses permitted by copyright law. For permission requests, write to the publisher, at the address below.

La Luna Press, L.L.C.
P.O. Box 533284
Indianapolis, IN
46253
USA

Thank you for purchasing this book.

For more information,
please visit us at:

www.lalunapress.com

Thank you to my dear family for their never-ending love and support:
Amy, David, Debbie, Diane, Hope, John, Johnny, Kristi, Marjorie, Megan, Wayne

Thank you also to my dear friends:

A, A, B, R, M, X, P, C, L, S

Finally, to my dear friend Sally.

Rest in peace my dear friend.

See you in the moon.

Table of Contents:

Thank You..	1
Sensitive...	2
Three Little Words............................	2
I Wish..	3
I'm Tired...	4
Loneliness...	5
Afraid to Love..................................	5
Language of Love............................	6
Solo Vs. Solo...................................	7
I Meant to Tell You.........................	8
I Love to Sing..................................	9
The Wall around My Heart...............	10
Dreams..	11
They Are All I Will Never Be............	12
I Miss You..	12
To the Men Who Have Hurt Me.......	13
To the Man I Will Love.....................	14
Metamorphosis.................................	15
Everyone Deserves a Chance to Fly..	15
Goodbye...	16
Life Lessons.....................................	17
I am Hope..	18
The Love of a Friend.......................	18
I am a Poet......................................	19
I'm Not Blue, I'm Indigo..................	19
Honorable Mention...........................	21
A Journey to the Moon.....................	21
Thoughts about Writing....................	22
It's Quiet in the Library Today..........	23
Words of Hope.................................	24
Painted White Face..........................	25
A Phoenix..	26
Fourteen Seagulls.............................	27
Between Yesterday and Today..........	28
A Work in Progress..........................	29
Inspiration..	30
Never Forget....................................	31
Friendship..	33
6 Months..	33

One in Seven....................................	34
Love...	35
One Year...	36
Masterpiece......................................	37
Thoughts about Love.......................	38
Best Friends.....................................	39
The Power of Words........................	40
Through My Eyes.............................	41
A Wonderful Sight to See................	42
Lessons from 2011...........................	43
Seriously?...	45
Changes..	46
Postcard from the Moon..................	47
A Magical Night...............................	48
I'm Home..	50
Milestones..	51
Writer's Block..................................	51
Lies..	52
Dear Moon..	54
Let the Magic Begin.........................	55
Daydreams..	56
My Indigo Knight.............................	57
A Year Later.....................................	58
Dear Sally...	60
Milestone Birthday..........................	61
Life..	62
What I Want Out of Life..................	62
Greater Than, Less Than, Equal To..	63
Gone Too Soon.................................	65
Poet of the Moon.............................	66
Mirrors..	66
The Keeper of the Key.....................	67
When My Cat Howls........................	68
The Death of a Friendship...............	69

I am Hope

Thank You 06/24/2010

*I wrote this poem for a person I once knew.

Thank you.....
...for reminding me of what I already know...for holding up the mirror to my face, making me see what I didn't know I wasn't seeing...making me see the reflection, even though I didn't like it...for listening to me...for hearing what I am saying, and what I am not...for challenging me...for making me feel safe enough to open my heart again...for making me acknowledge I have feelings...for making me tell you the truth about how I'm feeling, especially when I don't want to...for catching me stalling, when I didn't even know I was...for letting me cry, and it being okay to cry...for making me cry...for letting me be vulnerable...for always knowing the right thing to say...for making me feel...for understanding me...for being sweet to me...for your talent, at everything you do...for making me feel amazed when I think about you...for your wisdom...for your intellect...for your humor...for your poetry...for your passion...for your artistry...for always being able to make me laugh...for letting me show you the real me...for seeing me, the real me, and liking what you see...for being as fascinated with me as I am with you...for knowing I exist...for sharing things with me...for inspiring me to write again...for reading this poem...for being my friend.

Thank you.

Sensitive   08/14/2010

If there is a word that describes me, sensitive would be it.

My mind.
My skin.
My face.
My stomach.
My thoughts.
My perceptions.
My feelings.
My heart.
My emotions.
Me.
I am sensitive.

Three Little Words   09/26/2010

Three little words. What power they have. Three little words. I've not heard them before. Well, I've heard them before...but not directed at me. Not by someone outside my family. Not by someone outside my family who actually means it. The power of words. They can make you feel so special, so accepted, so understood, so cared about, so validated. WOW. To think that someone actually thinks that of me...and that I hear these Three Little Words...often...when I hadn't heard them at all. WOW. What a great feeling. All that caring, compassion, friendship in Three Little Words.

I WISH   2010

I wish my life were different-in a good way.

I wish I could be as kind, generous and supportive of myself as I am to others.

I wish I could look in the mirror and see me.

I wish I could see the value of my talents, and all the contributions I make to the world.

I wish my wing wasn't broken. I wish I didn't feel loneliness.

I wish I would not get sick of myself.

I wish love would find me.

I wish I would give myself a break.

I wish I would give myself the concern and respect that others don't give me.

I wish I wasn't so sensitive-inside and out.

I wish I felt comfortable in confiding my feelings.

I wish I could take off my mask. I wish I would tell myself, "You are enough."

I wish I could tell you what I really want to tell you.

I wish I were someone else. For just a day.

I wish I could be-me.

I'M TIRED   08/15/2010

I'm tired:
- ...of trying to live up to the expectations of others
- ...of being unappreciated
- ...of worrying about my parents
- ...of worrying
- ...of cancer
- ...of existing, not living
- ...of letting fear rule my life
- ...acting like nothing is wrong, especially when it is
- ...of only coming home to a cat
- ...of being alone
- ...of not being loved
- ...of thinking I will never be loved
- ...of thinking I will never find love
- ...of thinking I'm missing something (If I have never been loved, I can't miss it, now can I?)
- ...of not having anyone to hold me close and tell me everything will be alright
- ...of not having someone to spend time with, do things with
- ...of not expressing my feelings, even though I'm terrified to do so
- ...of the world not seeing the real me
- ...of not letting the world see the real me
- ...of being afraid to confide
- ...of being afraid
- ...of constantly patching and maintaining the wall around my heart
- ...of being tired.

I'm tired.

Loneliness   09/20/2010

Loneliness. How can one be lonely when one has known love? For those of us that have never known love, never experienced love, will never know love, it brings a different understanding, or definition to loneliness.

Afraid to Love   10/03/2010

My friend said this phrase yesterday, in conversation, about her own life. As soon as she said it, the words reverberated in my brain. "Afraid to Love." I had never heard of such a concept before. It makes total sense, hearing her story and knowing mine. I didn't know it at the time, but I now know that I am afraid to love. It is one of the few things in life that I long for-I long for it with every fiber of my being. But I am scared of it. I am afraid to love. The second I heard that phrase, I thought, "That is YOU. You are AFRAID TO LOVE."

I then asked myself, "But why are you afraid to love?" The answer immediately popped in my head-"You are afraid of being hurt again. Friends and boyfriends have hurt you. It makes total sense to be afraid of being hurt again."

But then the other answer popped in my head-"You are also afraid of not being loved in return. The two men you loved-or that you thought you loved-didn't love you. Why risk all the time and effort and being hurt into people that don't share those feelings of love?

If you keep the gate to the wall shut to keep out the hurt, you are also keeping out the chance of love. Love might have a key to enter the gate, it might not. The mask you wear-every day-it is just another wall. It is a coping mechanism. A defense mechanism. But, remember that line from that movie, 'Some things in some people are worth it.'

This discovery is not a panacea, not an instant cure. But as you are afraid to feel, to take off the mask, to let people in, to let people see the real you, and to let people know you, the real you, you are also afraid to love. Had you ever experienced love, or been showed love, you would know what a miraculous thing you are missing."

The Language of Love   01/08/2011

I heard a phrase in a song the other day-"the language of love."

I began to think about the different words in this language, spoken and not, and the concepts of this language, spoken and not.

I have heard this language before.

I could speak a few words, but I didn't have an understanding of this language.

I still don't.

There are many words, concepts, thoughts, idioms, nouns, adjectives, adverbs and verbs in this language.

I have yet to do so, but with every fiber of my being, I would love to learn the language of love.

I am Hope

Solo vs. Solo   01/23/2011

I've learned that learning Spanish in a single word-"solo"- translates into two words with different meanings. This word can be translated as "alone" and "lonely." Let me use each word in a sentence:

"Living as single woman means doing many things alone."
"Vivir como mujer soltera significa hacer muchas cosas solo."

"The woman felt lonely when her friend didn't come over for dinner."
"La mujer sintió solo cuando su amigo no vino a cenar."

Being alone can be a good thing. Living the single life, not having to answer to anyone, going anywhere you want, whenever you want, or not going anywhere, can be very liberating. As you told me, being alone cares for you and protects you. However, being alone may keep others out. Being alone may also be a bad thing-you have no one to go places with, trust, and share your life with.

Being alone can, and often does, lead to other emotions, feelings of loneliness. For me, when I have to talk to someone and I cannot, for whatever reason, it makes me feel lonely. When I see couples in the street and crave the love that I have never found, that makes me feel lonely. When I feel that there is no one on Earth but me, that makes me feel lonely. When I need to talk to someone-anyone-and I cannot, makes me feel lonely.

In my opinion, these two words and their definitions are very different. Being alone is to be by yourself, whether by consequences or choice. Being lonely is being alone and sad. How ironic that these two words, with these definitions being polar opposite, translate into the same word.

I am Hope

I Meant to Tell You   02/14/2011

I meant to tell you
...you told me...I meant to tell you
...I don't know why I didn't tell you
...I guess I forgot to tell you...I wanted to tell you
...and I'm so glad I can tell you...and that you can tell me
...and that I can tell you
...and that I can feel secure enough to tell you
....what I meant to tell you...and I guess I forgot to tell you
...but I really want to tell you
...and I can't believe I get to tell you
.......what I've wanted to tell you
...at first I remember it was hard to tell you
...because no one had told it to me, how could I tell you
...but now someone tells it to me-you
...I really should tell you...usually, you tell it to me
...before I get a chance to tell you
...but I have to tell you...I want to tell you
...especially today,
....I have to tell you
...well, I want to tell you...
             ....I love you.

"I Love You" in American Sign Language

I Love to Sing   02/23/2011

I love to sing. I love that people are shocked when they hear my voice-they can't believe it's me. I love seeing this shock on people's faces turn into a smile.

I love that my Mom wants to have a CD of Handel's Messiah, all 3 parts, with just my voice. I love to challenge myself in singing.

I love that I can sing very quietly, just above a whisper, and that I can sing loudly enough to fill a room.

I love that when I sing "Caledonia" my cat stares in me, in total awe, as if to say, "How do you do that?!?"

I love that I can express myself through my singing.

I love that I can express my emotions, and emotions that aren't even mine. I love to sing in funny ways, in different accents or voices, to make someone laugh. I love that when I sing along to another singer, I can change my voice to imitate theirs.

I can be anyone I want to be. I love that I can actually turn heads when people hear me sing. I love that with my voice I can soar high above the clouds with the other angels, even with my broken wing.

I love that my voice can shock, stun, touch, impress, inspire, awe, and move people to tears.

I love that you cried when I sang you an Italian aria. I love to sing, even though no one else will hear me.

I love to sing.

The Wall around My Heart   02/26/2011

There is a wall around my heart that shelters me and protects me. This wall has stood for years. It has seen several periods of building up and tearing down. While the purpose of this wall is to keep me safe, away from harm, it also isolates me and keeps me from knowing people. It keeps me away from friendship. It keeps me away from love. It makes me feel unhappy, isolated, and lonely.

The wall is constructed after a new hurt. A deep, devastating hurt. The wall is very easy to put up; it is built brick by brick. It protects me, keeps my secrets, shields me from harm and keeps me from getting hurt. It comforts me to know I am protected. But, at what cost? The wall has been known to have armed guards around the wall. It's even had electrical fencing installed on the top, for further protection.

As the wall goes up, brick by brick, the wall also comes down brick by brick. As I come to know someone, and as someone comes to know me, the bricks are chipped out of the wall. When I share a funny story-that's a brick. When I share a secret-brick. When I confide my feelings-brick. When I share a hurt-brick. When I trust someone-brick. One by one. Brick by brick.

There is a wall around my heart. It is now at a height where one can step over it and access my heart within. That is, if I let myself let you in.

Dreams   04/02/2011

Once upon a time I received an autographed photo of a celebrity. The celebrity had signed their name, and had also written, "May all your dreams come true." I thought about that phrase over and over. "May all your dreams come true." May all my dreams come true. That made me think, "My dreams....my dreams?!?", as if.

I didn't understand the concept. That made me think, "Well, what are my dreams?" I realized that I wasn't having fun in life- I was being efficient. I wasn't living, I was existing. I hadn't realized it, but life had taken over. Life had taken over, and had taken all of my dreams-without my consent-and I hadn't even realized it. And that is sad. I decided from that point on to think about what I wanted, to actually make new dreams. The same things kept coming into my head-"Get a better job", "Meet a nice man", "Fall in Love", "Get Married." But then what? Say I do get a better job, meet a nice man, fall in love, and get married. Say all of these "dreams" come true. But then what? That's not the end of the story-that's not the end of my story. Happily ever after, if it exists, is not the end of my story. Now that I can dream, now I have the power to dream, I don't know what to dream. I don't even know if I'm brave enough to dream. Dreams can be so powerful, so magical, so liberating, so wonderful. But those are dreams that come true. The dreams do not come true, or can't become a reality can be fraught with rejection, disappointment, hurt, pain. "May all your dreams come true." How can they come true when I haven't even dreamt them yet? I didn't know that the world is open to me. As a friend once said, "Everything is Possible." My life is just now allowing the possibility of believing in dreams again. Life is letting me dare to think about a dream that might or might not come true-if I dare be brave enough to dream it. But not before. Life had taken over, and had taken all of my dreams-without my consent-and I hadn't even realized it. And that is sad.

They Are All I Will Never Be   04/02/2011

Have you ever looked at the life of someone else, a celebrity, an artist, a filmmaker, a performer, and seen all of their fantastic qualities? Then did you turn that vision inward on yourself? Were you disappointed with what you saw? Were you disillusioned with the comparison? Comparing yourself to others creates many thoughts in a person's head:-"Wow-their work is amazing." -"How did they do that?!?"-"God she is beautiful."-"I would kill for that hair."-"Look at her porcelain skin."-"That performance was incredible."-"That was so clever!"-"I wish I'd said that."-"I wish I'd said that first."-"I can't do that."-"I wish I could do that."-"I wish I could be that."-"I could never do that."-"That was hysterical!"-"That moved me to tears."-"That was amazing."-"That piece was amazing."-"It must be wonderful to be them."-"I wish I was them."-"I wish I was anyone else but me."-"They are all I will never be."

I Miss You   04/06/2011

I can't believe you're gone. You've been gone a week. An entire week. I feel like I just found out yesterday. I feel like this is some horrible, nasty dream, and that you are alive and well and cancer free. But sadly, that is the nasty dream, not reality. I wish I could talk to you one last time. I wish I could get your feedback on things. I wish I could hear your thoughts on the letters I sent.
I wish I could receive a birthday card from you. When I talked to you last week, I felt such comfort afterwards. But life goes on, as cruel a reality as that is. I miss sending you letters. I miss being able to communicate with you whenever I want. I can hear your voice. I can hear your laugh. I can see your smile. My heart is broken that you have left us. I never thought you would actually go. But I know that you are in heaven, watching all of us trying to deal with our grief of losing you. I know you are now pain free, and free to fly wherever you choose. Please forgive me for my selfishness in wishing you were here. It is just because I love you. I love you Sally. And I miss you.

To the Men Who Have Hurt Me   04/08/2011

To the men who have hurt me, I write this in the hopes of gaining closure, and freeing myself, once and for all. I am saddened when I look back on my friendship with you. I am saddened that I blamed myself for your mistakes. I am saddened that I obliterated my self-esteem and sense of self-worth rather than make you accountable for your own actions. You are the reason there is a wall around my heart. You are the reason that I, for years, harbored distrust in men.

I do not forgive you for your deception. I do not forgive you for your lies. I do not forgive you for hurting me. I do not forgive you for not telling the truth, because telling the truth "would hurt me." I do not forgive you for taking your friendship away from me without my consent.

I can never forgive you for the things that you have done to me. But, strange as it is, I can forgive you. Forgiving you frees me from the pain. Forgiving you allows me to let go of the hurt.

I will not carry this hurt anymore. If I hold on to the hurt, that gives you power. I am through giving you my power. I thank you for all you have taught me, even though you devastated me in the process.

I thank you for making me the woman I am today, self-reliant, capable of feeling emotion, confident. I thank you for getting the hell out of my life.

You should see me now.

You would never recognize me.

To the Man I Will Love   04/09/2011

To the man I will love: I have not met you yet, but I know you will change my life forever.

I know you will make me feel things in a way I have never felt before.

I know you will open my heart, and that I will never be the same.

I know I will share my heart with you, my life with you. I will be there for you, rejoicing in your triumphs, mourning your sorrows, helping you face challenges as they arise, giving you strength in times of adversity, giving you unending support.

I will love you unabashedly with all of my heart. I will be your friend, your partner, your confidant, your lover. I will be your champion, your captive audience, your biggest fan.

I will make you laugh when you are sad. I will hold your hand when you need support.

I will hug you when you need comfort. I will hold you close when you need my love.

I will let you in, behind the wall around my heart. I will tell you whatever is on my mind, especially when I don't want to.

I will let you see my pain. I will let you see my tears. I will let you see me cry.

I will let you dry my tears. I will let you hold me in your arms and comfort me.

I will share my laughter, tears, hopes, fears, thoughts, dreams and more.

Metamorphosis 04/17/2011

Thank you for teaching me that it is a good thing to have emotions, to express myself, that it is okay to be sad when I feel sad, for teaching me to cry and weep with happiness, for teaching me to never waste a single tear. Thank you for always listening, and for helping me remove my mask. Thank you for helping me to grow and blossom and change and become the person I am today. Me.

Everyone Deserves a Chance to Fly 04/20/2011

I am like the other woman whose name starts with E. I am mistaken, misunderstood. I am not as the world perceives me to be. I have been given a great power. And I am learning to use it. I have learned to be true to myself and who I am. I have learned to not hide myself, or negate my talents. I have learned that I am beautiful. I have learned to not stop being myself, even for a second. I have even learned to fly. Be it on a broom or my own wings, I have learned to fly. The view from the heights is breathtaking. From above, things take on a whole new perspective. The world is so beautiful. My vision is so much clearer. I can now see things I overlooked before. I can now see things I never would have been able to see otherwise, in the world before me and within. I see beauty. I see laughter. I see truth. I see love. I see me. I am grateful I have been taught to spread my wings and fly. Now that I have learned I hope I never stop. The wizard was right-everyone deserves a chance to fly.

Goodbye   04/26/2011

It has been a month since you left us.

I can't believe it has been a month. I think of you often.

At times I laugh, thinking of something funny you said, or the way you said it.

At times I cry, filled with deep sadness, missing you.

This is the hardest thing I have ever done.

This is breaking my heart. I don't want to do it, but I feel I should.

I cannot be selfish and hold on to you. You need to be free to fly with the other angels.

You have changed my life. I am going to miss you forever.

You will forever be my angel.

I will think of you and smile.

I will think of you and cry.

I love you Sally.

Goodbye.

Life Lessons   5/02/2011

Always take your sunglasses, even on a cloudy day.
Make sure you have your medicine.
Always keep a diet soda and chocolate on hand.
Open up your heart-you never know who will find their way in.
Be who you are-the good the bad and the ugly.
Let others be who they are.
Never relinquish your power.
Never stop dreaming.
Never stop hoping.
Do not hide who you are or what you are feeling.
Never be ashamed for being who you are.
Never be afraid to express yourself.
Make sure your loved ones know how you feel about them.
Cherish your friends.
Be forgiving and understanding of others, especially when they
    don't live up to your expectations.
Do not judge others harshly.
Embrace your freedom.
Stop to look at a sunset, or a rainbow.
Don't be afraid to let others in.
Never let anyone make you feel bad about yourself, who you are,
    what you are feeling.
Look in the mirror at yourself until you can see you-not your
    flaws.
Love how you look and your body-wrinkles, curves, cellulite and
    more. This is the only body you will ever get.
Stand up to fear.
Do not let fear stop you from realizing your dreams.
You will be hurt, very deeply. But you will survive.
Forgive those who have hurt you.
You have worth. You are enough.
You are beautiful. Love yourself.
Believe in yourself. Believe in love.
Believe

I am Hope   05/15/2011

I am Hope. I illuminate the darkness. I make the hard times a little easier. I make such a difference in your life, if you let me. Don't ever lose me. Find me. Hold on to me. Cling to me. Let me help you through the pain. If you need me, just seek me out.
I am always here for you. Trust in me. If you've lost me, find me. I'm never far.

"True hope is swift, and flies with swallows' wings;
Kings it makes gods, and meaner creatures kings."
-William Shakespeare, Richard III, Act V, scene ii

The Love of a Friend   06/16/2011

The love of a friend............
    ...can fill you up with the greatest joy...can brighten up even a perfect day...can make you happy that they e-mailed you, before you've even opened their message...can inspire you to learn new things...can inspire you to learn about them...can give you the courage to do things you never thought you could...can fill your soul with pure joy...can make you cry from pure joy...can love you when you don't love yourself...can make you see the beauty that others see in you...can remind you of what a wonderful person you are...can open up your world...can make you love the moon...can make you see one another without telescopes...can bring you endless possibilities...can make you share your deepest secrets...can make you tear down the wall around your heart...can make you take off your mask and let people in...can break your heart when you lose it...can fill you up when you've found it...can be the purest love you have ever known...can make you melt like ice in the sun...can teach you how to fly...can make you so very happy...can remind you that you're still you.

I Am a Poet 7/04/2011

I am a poet. I have been called many things over the years, many things I won't repeat. I am a daughter, a sister, an aunt, a co-worker, a person. I am a poet. And with my poetry I can fly. I am soaring above the Earth, marveling at its beauty. I can show you my heart and bare my soul, all this and more. For I am a poet.

"The Life of a Writer" by Esperanza Habla

I'm Not Blue, I'm Indigo 07/13/2011

The color indigo. The color of the midnight sky. The color that blue and violet make. The color indigo.

One day, when I was feeling, oh, let's say less than happy, I told a friend I was feeling blue. This friend said to me, "You're not blue, you're indigo."

At first I thought this friend was teasing me. I thought, "Yeah right, how can a person be indigo?" I was so curious, in fact, that I began to research just how a person can be indigo.

Some traits of an indigo person are: wise, insightful, spiritually aware, intuitive, perceptive, devoted, just, fair, responsible, and devoted to the truth.

Maybe I don't have these traits. But, maybe I *do* have these traits. Perhaps the greatest trait of an indigo person is introspection. That is one trait of being an indigo person that I will admit to. Through expressing myself through my writing, this has created great introspection.

I cannot write, create, without introspection. Thinking about things deeply, feeling things deeply, letting myself feel things deeply, that is how.

I create. That is how I am learning to live. That is how I am learning to breathe. That is how I learned to fly. My wings are a deep indigo color, made iridescent by the light of the moon.

My friend was right-I'm not blue, I'm indigo.

"Indigo Orchid" by Esperanza Habla

Honorable Mention   07/14/2011

A month or so ago I entered a writing contest at my workplace. I submitted my entry and, over the course of that month, I forgot all about the contest. Until today. I received an e-mail that my entry earned an Honorable Mention. My submission-an Honorable Mention. It is the first time as a writer that I have won anything.

I am not going to have my picture in the paper, I am not going to meet the mayor. (I did win a $25 gift card though.) But, honestly, I don't care. I won Honorable Mention. If you were to ask me how I feel right now-honored.
And very proud.

A Journey to the Moon   07/21/2011

I'm about to embark on a journey- a journey to the Moon.

I don't know what I'm going to find there…rocks, footprints from astronauts past…

I've never been to the Moon before-I'm a little nervous about it.

That being said, I cannot wait to see the beauty of the Earth from up high in the sky….

…..to see the wonders that can only be seen from a vantage point in the moon.

Thoughts about Writing   07/23/2011

When inspiration strikes I sit at a computer or with paper and pen, I just sit and write. I give myself the freedom to write whatever comes to mind. When I write I go into a zone. It's like I'm not in control anymore. My heart knows what I want to say, and my fingers write it. I just sit there, letting the thoughts flow. I don't know when I'm done with the poem until I'm done writing. After I've written something I'll take a step back, go do something else for a while. I will come back to the poem and scrutinize what I've written. If I think it's good, I will get it ready to publish. If I read it and it is garbage, I will discard it. I have not had this blog a long time, only 5 months. But in that time I have gotten such sincere, positive feedback about my poetry. To be honest, I am surprised that other people think I am a talented writer. I remember saying, "Really? Me? You really think I have talent in my writing?" I was astonished. I never thought that I had any talent at being a writer. I'm beginning to think otherwise. At first, I saw my poetry as a way for me to express myself, what I am thinking and feeling. I was astonished to hear how my poetry speaks to people, how it connects with people on an emotional level.

I am amazed that people are so moved by what I write. That is a great feeling. I have received many comments from people regarding my writing, everything from "Your heart shown through the screen" to "It is beautiful, like you." There have been many comments, with one comment in common-"Keep writing." I don't know what my literary future is, or what wonders my writing will bring to my life. But, I have a feeling that the world will open up to me in a way it never has before. As a friend once told me, I should keep writing, because....
  "the world needs more Hope."

I am Hope

It's Quiet in the Library Today   08/09/2011

It's quiet in the library today. Believe it or not, that is a rare commodity these days-for a library to actually be quiet. There's usually always the sounds of the hustle and bustle of patrons looking for their holds, patrons talking to their neighbor, or catching up with a long lost friend, a patron yelling at library staff because they have a fine and don't want to pay it, children running here and there, excited about finding a book they want to read, or fighting with their siblings about which movie they're going to watch first when they get home, babies shrieking at the top of their lungs, the way only babies can, the clatter of cases being opened to get the CDs and movies out of them, the thud of materials dropping into the return bin, the copier running in its usual whir of machinery, the buzz of the printer making printouts of hold notices, the beeps of the lasers as we process the returned materials....all of these noises, heard all at once, can be a deafening symphony.

But not today. The library is blissfully, joyfully, peacefully quiet. A person can relax and actually read a book if they want to.

A person can relax with a latte and read the morning paper if they want to.

A person can hear themselves think, for the library is blissfully at peace.

It's quiet in the library today.

"The Library" by Esperanza Habla

Words of Hope　　　　　　　　　　　　08/12/2011

I heard this phrase the other day-Words of Hope. That phrase has stuck in my mind-Words of Hope. This blog is called Esperanza, which, in Spanish, means "Hope". My pseudonym is Esperanza Habla, which, in Spanish, means "Hope Speaks." This blog could almost be called "Words of Hope"-after all, you are reading my words, and that is my name.

One thing I keep hearing form my readers is "keep writing." It means so much to know that something I wrote means something to another person. When I began writing, I never thought that I had any talent at writing-it was just something I did to express myself. After I began writing, and began this blog, it was then private. I later shared my poems with a local author. He encouraged me to make my blog public. He pointed out that, through this blog, through my poetry...maybe I can help someone through a difficult time in their life.

Maybe I can inspire someone to write something of their own. Maybe I can help someone feel better, on a stressful day. To date I have had over 1,800 visits to this blog. That is astounding to me. Thank you, my readers, for coming back to my blog every now and again, to see what is new on the site, See what thoughts I've put on the blog.

I truly appreciate your support in this new creative outlet of mine. It makes me feel good to know that my words have meant something to you...that you have encouraged me to keep writing, that you care enough to read the *Words of Hope*.

Painted White Face 08/15/2011

*I dedicate this poem to my mime friends around the world

There is a din in the room. The lights are dimmed. The audience goes silent. The stage lights brighten. The spotlight shines on a person on stage. A man-dressed in black, with white gloves, and a painted white face. The man stands motionless. The music starts. The artist begins to move.

Worlds are created through hands in gloves. Gestures translate into words unspoken. Feelings are conveyed with the face, the body. Feelings are felt with the heart, with the soul.

Smiles can appear from nowhere. Tears can fall like rain. Sorrows can broaden. Joys can greaten. Hearts can break. Hearts can mend. Souls can be made clean.

The air is carved with movement. Movement is poetry in motion. With every breath, every sigh, with every gesture, every glance, with every nuance of movement the world is made more beautiful. The performer ends his performance, once again motionless. The audience remains still-in a state of rapture, in a state of awe, struck by the radiance, struck by the beauty-the beauty they've seen, the beauty that remains.

The audience erupts in applause, erupts in cheers-cheers for the performance they've just seen, for the performance they have been privileged to see. The artist on stage bows to thank the audience for their part, the applause for a job well done.

All of these feelings, all of these emotions, the laughter, the tears...from an experience they've had...the experience of seeing a master perform their art. All of that from the performer on stage, with white gloves, and a painted white face.

I am Hope

A Phoenix 8/16/2011

Phoenix, the mythical bird that lives, is consumed in flames, and begins anew.

A time of death, a time of rebirth.

The phoenix.

Pulls itself out of the flames, rises from the ashes.

Wills itself to begin anew.

Does not dwell on what has been, only on what will be.

I have known the fire, and felt its burn.

This is *my* time. My time to shine. My time to fly.

I have risen from the ashes and am living anew, breathing anew, cleaning the ashes off my wings.

I feel like a phoenix.

"The bird proudly willing to burn,
So that he may live again,
Chooses the flames of fires
That burn the aged Phoenix
The nature stands still
Till a new young bird starts again,
and begins the legend of the Phoenix
**   - Claudian (Roman author)**

Fourteen Seagulls   08/21/2011

I was driving to the local grocery store today, not five minutes from my house.

I arrived at the store, found a parking spot, and parked my car.

I got out of the car and heard a strange sound. It was a caw.

I recognized that sound. I thought to myself...

"I couldn't have just heard a caw. Seagulls make a caw sound. I remember that sound, from the sea. Seagulls make that sound. I couldn't have just heard a caw."

Just then I heard another caw.

I turned my head in the direction the sounds came from. There, in the distance, were 14 seagulls. I counted them to make sure.

14 seagulls.

Milling around the parking lot, looking for food.

My home is thousands of miles away from the ocean. I thought to myself...

"What are they doing here? They are so out of place."

My next thought was...

"Maybe they are the ones that are supposed to be here.

Maybe _we_ are the ones out of place."

Between Yesterday and Today   08/24/2011

Yesterday was a different day. It seems, looking back,
I went through my day sleeping while awake. I existed,
I didn't live. I had a heart closed off by hurt. My heart was heavy,
filled with rejection and distrust. But not today.

Today is a different day. I have awakened refreshed. Overnight
has been a metamorphosis. I am not the same person. I have
awakened with a new vision. I have found my voice. I am singing
so that others can hear me. I am being heard. I am finding skills
and abilities that were asleep in me-abilities I never knew I had.

As I have opened my heart, to let in love, the world has shown
me its beauty. I have found my wings, and have taken flight. The
views from this height are breathtaking. The flight is thrilling.
I never want to stop soaring. In looking back to yesterday,
I don't recognize myself. Today I am a different person.
A phoenix with indigo wings. There has been such a difference,
such a change, such a metamorphosis. You wouldn't believe the
changes that I see, between yesterday and today.

"Between Yesterday and Today" by Esperanza Habla

A Work in Progress   08/29/2011

I was thinking about my dreams. I'm glad I'm beginning to let myself dream. I have a small list, but a sincere list. So, here are some of my dreams:

To fall in love. To get married. To love and to be loved forever. To be a published poet. To be a published author. To earn a living from my literary projects. To move to another city in a warmer climate. To travel to Peru. To live a life dedicated to the arts. To find happiness. Total happiness. For my dreams to come true, and for me to cherish every moment of it.

I don't know if my dreams will come true. I don't know if that's all of my dreams. I don't know if I can dream more dreams, and make a new list as I go along.

That's what I'm going to do. I'm going to make a new list as I go along. If a dream came true, wonderful. If not, I will add it to the new list. It seems like my list of dreams, like life, is a work in progress.

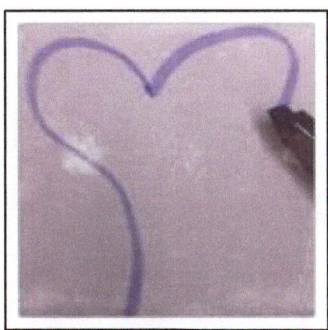

"Work in Progress" by Esperanza Habla

Inspiration   09/01/2011

Inspiration is elusive. It can happen when you least suspect it. Just like love.

Inspiration is hard to find. I don't think it's anything a person can actively search for, it just happens. Just like love.

You can spend your days looking for it, making yourself miserable trying to find it.

But when the stars align, and when the time is right, inspiration comes to you. Just like love.

I don't think we find inspiration, it finds us. When we least suspect it, when we're not even looking for it, it finds us. Just like love.

Don't look for it. Let it find you.

Inspiration can come in a thought, a moment, a line in a song, a quote from a movie, a word from a best friend.

It then starts a chain reaction, an aligning of thoughts and feelings-a mixture of thoughts and emotions that come together and live as one. Just like two people in love.

The result of this inspiration-the thought, the poem, the sonnet, the movie, the song, can fill your heart with the greatest joy, the greatest bliss. Just like love.

Inspiration is just like love.

Once you've found it, you just know.

Never Forget   09/08/2011

I remember that day, as many people do. I got up, bathed, and turned on the TV, to listen to the news, as I regularly do.

I remember putting on my clothes, and as I did so I heard the anchor on the national morning show say that a second plane had just hit. I thought to myself, "What?!?!??"

I then went into the living room and began to watch. I sat in rapt attention, as did many around the world. I sat there, spellbound, unable to process what was happening.

I was so engrossed that I was almost late to work. I remember feeling like I didn't want to leave the house. I had to know what was going on.

I arrived to work barely on time. I found my boss counting money and watching television-on the TV usually used to show movies to children in the summertime. Before we opened that morning, the first tower fell.

I remember that when we opened that morning, we brought the TV out so our patrons could keep up to date with everything. So *we* could keep up to date on everything.

Later in the day I remember watching the news coverage in between patrons. I then had a patron come in who was quite chipper-in total contradiction to the day. She spoke about what a great day she was having, about the weather, this that and the other.

She then noticed I wasn't saying anything back to her. I had been listening, not wanting to interrupt. She then asked me how I was. I told her I was ok. She asked me why I was just ok. I said, "Haven't you seen the news?" The woman replied,
"Oh yeah. My Father is supposed to be on one of the planes."

I am Hope

I then understood why she was so talkative and chipper-she was in denial. The reality of the situation hadn't hit her yet.

She kept talking and talking and talking, more manic with every minute that passed. The more she spoke, in her mind, the more she kept the horror of the reality at bay.

It was if, if she stopped talking, it would confirm her worst fears. It would make it true.

I was lucky. I didn't lose anyone that day.

I don't know anyone that lost anyone that day. In New York, Pennsylvania or Washington D.C.

I was also lucky in that I was busy working. I didn't see much of the horrors of that day, even though we did have the TV on.

I learned two important life lessons that day:

First-that we as a people are strong.

>   I don't mean Americans, I mean people.

>   People are fighting for their freedoms,
>   against injustice and tyranny, all over the world.

>   We as a people are strong.

Second-freedom isn't free.

Friendship   2011

Friendship means...
    ...rejoicing in one another's triumphs...sharing one another's sorrows...being there when they need you...letting them be there when you need them...accepting one another unconditionally for who and what they are...to never judge one another...offering a hug in celebration...holding their hand in support...to share one another's laughter and their tears...being there for one another in times of adversity...giving one another chance when they've hurt you...to put hurt feelings aside in time of need...to give one another their space when they need it...to put their needs first before your own...to forgive one another, not necessarily what they've done ...to think of one another and smile...to offer a kind word when they're hurting...sharing the truth with one another, no matter how painful...being respectful of one another...being honest with one another...be caring to one another...being kind to one another...loving one another...
    ....being a friend.

6 Months   09/30/2011

I can't believe it's been six months. I can't believe you left us six months ago. I think of you often, Sally. You will be in my heart forever. I miss you. I love you.

One In Seven   10/01/2011

I think, as we find life's little twists and turns, bumps in the road, we come across a person we want to help, an organization we want to donate our time to, a charity we write a check to support, or just a cause that is near and dear to our hearts. For me, that cause is breast cancer.

Here in the US, where I live, October is National Breast Cancer Awareness Month. Pink ribbons are to be found everywhere-on products, in stores, even the clothing we wear, all to help bring awareness of this killer disease. That is why this blog, for the month of October, will be pink.

The statistic for women to be diagnosed with breast cancer was one out of every eight women. Now the statistic is one in seven. The number of breast cancer patients is increasing, not decreasing.

Think about it-one in seven women. Look around you. If you have seven female friends, who will it be? If there are seven women in your family, ask yourself-which one will it be? There are seven women in my family. In my family, it was my Mother who got breast cancer. Her cancer was discovered years ago. It was caught quickly, and was at a very low stage of growth. I'm sure that is why my Mother is here today to tell her tale. That and her excellent course of treatment.

If you are a woman, do your monthly breast examinations. They can save your life. Get mammograms. Love yourself enough to take care of yourself. You are the only you there will ever be.

If you are a man, be aware that men can get breast cancer as well. Urge the women in your life to take care of themselves.

Love   10/01/2011

*I wrote this poem for a friend who had a broken heart.
I now dedicate it to everyone with a broken heart.*

I know you have been hurting. I know that you have been looking for love, and have not found the love for you, the perfect one, your forever love. You have been hurt in your search. The ones that have loved you have left you.

Don't give in to the hurt. Don't give up. You must stay strong. There is a love for you that will be a forever love. It will challenge you, make you grow, make you question what you believe.

I know it is hard, looking for love and always coming up empty, wanting someone to share your joys, sorrows, to embrace you, to comfort you, to love you. Love will find you. When you least suspect it, love will find you.

Your love is coming. Your love will be immediate and instantaneous. It will be all encompassing. It will be a forever love. And the pain you felt searching for this love, the hurt that others inflicted upon you, it will go away forever. It will be nothing more than a faint memory. You will be happy. Blissfully, endlessly happy.

I know there is a love for you out there, just as I know there is a love for me out there. You deserve to be happy. The perfect one for you will be sent to you. You will no longer be lonely. You will not feel the pain of rejection, the pain of others who did not care about your feelings. You will find love. I know there is a love for you out there. I know this with all of my heart. There is not a question in my mind.

You will find your forever love, your perfect one. When you find them, acknowledge the gift of their love. Be grateful to have found your love. Cherish every moment.

One Year   10/07/2011

I can't believe it's been one year. A year ago, approximately, I began writing. I was encouraged by some new friends to write down what I was thinking and feeling. When I look at myself a year ago, I don't recognize the person I used to be.

When I wrote my first poem, after years of not writing, I never dreamed I'd write another one, let alone create a blog of my poetry and share it with the world. I never thought the world would open up to me as I opened up my heart. I never thought that I would begin to dream again.

I never thought that any of my dreams would ever come true. I never thought that I would be taught to fly. I want to thank my dear friends B, A, A, M, P, C, J, S, S, and my family for your unending support and encouragement over the past year. Thank you for nurturing me, giving me the confidence to go forward, for believing in me when I didn't believe in myself.

Thank you, S, my friend and writing partner, for teaching me how to fly.

And to you, my dear friend Sally-Pooh; everything I ever write will be dedicated to you. Rest in peace, my dear friend.

As I sat down to begin writing this poem, I thought about how to even begin to talk about the things that can happen in a year. Babies are born, dear friends die. Friends are made, friends are lost.

Relationships are made, relationships fall apart. People are wed, people get divorced. But there's a better way to measure everything that can happen in a year-
      -in love.

Masterpiece 10/12/2011

As a new writer and poet, I have been thinking about the concept of a masterpiece.

A person's crowning achievement. The epitome of their work.

Something everyone can look upon and can instantly recognize it as being a masterpiece.

There is a famous saying that "beauty is in the eye of the beholder." Someone who may be devastatingly handsome may be a vile person, while a person who isn't much to look at on the outside can have the most beautiful soul you've ever seen.

When one thinks of the word "masterpiece," a work of art comes to mind. Maybe the painting of a famous artist.

However, I feel as with any painting, any sculpture, any classical piece of music, any work of art, this phrase is true-the beauty is in the eye of the beholder. What might speak to one person might not speak to another.

So please do not go looking for a masterpiece, as I have.

Open your eyes and your heart to the beauty around you.

The poem that helps you, the song that gives you peace of mind, the movie that gives you comfort, the poem that embodies who you are and what you feel, the painting that speaks to you, the way the piece of art makes you feel-*that is the masterpiece.*

Thoughts about Love   10/19/2011

There is a famous quote by Maya Angelou, about love that states: **"Love is like a virus. It can happen to anybody at any time."** I hope this is so.

I have had strong feelings for men, feelings that I thought were love. Actually, they were love-a variation of love-love amongst friends.

But not a forever love. Not the kind of love that makes you fall in love with someone and want to marry them and start a life with them.

I have never found love; love has never found me. Although I have never experienced love in the above definition, I believe that it exists.

I believe that love will find me-or I will find love. I have to believe that.

I have to hold on to that belief. If I don't believe that, what's the point?

I know that love exists. I've seen it. I've felt it. Maybe not in all of its incarnations, but I have felt it.

Since I know it exists, I have to believe that it is out there waiting for me.

Maybe, if I stop looking for love, it will find me. When the time is right.

Maybe that's how it's supposed to be.

Best Friends   10/20/2011

"Friendship is a single soul dwelling in two bodies"
- Aristotle

I have been thinking a lot about the concept of friendship, and more specifically, the concept of a "best friend." I have written an earlier poem about friendship, in which I wrote all of the qualities that I think go into a friendship. But the concept of a best friend is something different entirely.

I believe that everyone can have more than one best friend. I have a few best friends-A, A, B, R, S, and a few more people that I would identify as an initial. A friend is something that is best in quality, not quantity.

A best friend-that is someone who you can share your deepest darkest secrets with. The person you have a strong bond in friendship with. The person that knows how you're feeling without you even saying a word. The person that knows the meaning of your silence. The person that gives you a shoulder to cry on without you having to ask for one. The person that gives you the strongest hugs. The person that puts your needs before their own. The person that you can be totally honest with. The person that listens when you need to talk about something. The person that makes you laugh when you most need it. The person who brings out the best in you. The person that lets you be yourself and loves you as you are. The person that helps you evolve into the person you were meant to be.

-"A best friend is one who reaches for your hand but touches your heart."-Author Unknown

The Power of Words   10/26/2011

Words are a powerful thing.

Once they are given power, they can do anything.

Words can hurt-Words can heal
Words can damage-Words can comfort
Words can enrage a heart-Words can soften a soul
Words can outrage our sensibilities-Words can calm a spirit
Words can incite a riot-Words can calm a riot
Words can bring nations to war-Words can bring nations peace
Words can be aimed like an arrow-Words can float like a cloud
Words can be used as a weapon-Words can be used as a tool
Words can be ugly-Words can be beautiful
Words can devastate-Words can enlighten
Words can slice a heart in half-Words can make a heart whole
Words can crush a heart-Words can heal a spirit
Words can make you burst into tears-Words can make you burst
    into laughter
Words can tear you down-Words can lift you up
Words can discourage-Words can inspire
Words can break your heart-Words can fill your heart
Words can make you lose a love-Words can help you find a love
Words can hurt-Words can heal

Words are a powerful thing.

Once they are given power, they can do anything.

Through My Eyes   11/03/2011

In the past year I have begun to look at the world. Really see the world. See the world apart from me. It's amazing what I have seen, when I've taken the time to look through my eyes.

With my new found clarity, I have a vision like never before. I have seen the impact of the written word, with people I have never met. I have seen that as I have opened my heart, the world has opened itself to me. I have seen a beauty in the world, and in myself, that I've never seen before.

I can see that
- I am a complex creature with many thoughts and feelings
- I am a unique creation
- I am the only me there will ever be
- I have my own beauty specific to me
- I have a laugh that is all my own
- I am here for a purpose
- I am worthy of love
- I am worthy of being loved
- I am enough

All this lies within you too. It's right there. Open your eyes.

It's amazing what you'll find, if you take the time to look through your eyes.

A Wonderful Sight to See   11/22/2011

This afternoon, a precious sight caught my eye.

In the library where I work, there are several places for children to sit and read.

In one of these places, I saw two girls, sisters, sitting and reading a book.

The elder sister was reading the book to the younger sister.

The younger sister sat and listened attentively to the story while holding a stuffed animal, a horse (by the neck, almost in a hug) which looked every bit as big as the little girl herself.

I don't know what book the girls were reading, or where the adventure in the book had taken them.

To see the two girls sitting in one seat together, lost in a book, sharing reading a book together, it was a wonderful sight to see.

Lessons From 2011

I've been thinking about the past year. So much has happened. Babies have been born, friends have gotten married, friends have had their hearts broken, dear friends have died. Friendships have been made. Friendships have been lost. Friendships have been tested. I lost a dear friend this year. I almost lost another one.

I learned many lessons this year. Lessons about emotions, healing, honesty, respect, strength, trust, forgiveness.

While I didn't choose to receive these lessons, I am grateful for having learned all they taught me.

I learned that emotions, like words, can be used as weapons and must be used and treated with restraint.

I learned that the truth can hurt just as much as a lie.

I learned the immense power of forgiveness, for myself and others.

I learned that, no matter the crisis, I can survive it.

I have learned that I have reserves of strength that I didn't know even existed.

I learned that when we lose a friend or loved one due to death, they are never far away. They are forever in our hearts.

I learned that, while I have lost my voice, I have found another.

I learned that, when others have harmed me, to risk everything, open up my heart, and give them another chance. Some things, and some people, are worth it.

I have learned that Prince Charming is still slaying dragons, and won't be arriving for quite some time. I need to prepare to rescue myself, in case he never shows up.

I learned to put the needs of friends in need before my own.

I learned to not give up on those that love me, and most importantly, myself.

I learned once, while crying, thinking my heart was going to burst from grief, that a friend was going through a pain worse than mine. In helping that friend, I was able to help myself.

I learned that hearts are resilient. They can be easily crushed and can heal, given time.

I learned to not undervalue myself as a person and as a woman.

I learned that, although I have never experienced it, to never close my heart to the possibility of love.

I learned that any man would be a fool to not fall in love with me.

I learned that I am beautiful. I learned to love the moon.

I learned that I'm here. I'm alive.

I learned that I have so much more to learn.

I learned I can't wait for 2012.

Seriously?   01/04/2012

Since the New Year has begun, I've seen a barrage of weight loss commercials. Every weight loss company, product, diet, etc. has felt the need to sell their wares on television. The reason, it seems, is to help all of us-that are overweight-to finally overcome "the battle of the bulge" and lose weight. Commercials with success stories of weight loss are inspiring and empowering. However, in recent days I have seen at least 3 commercials on television for weight loss reduction companies that have women as their spokesperson-women who have never had a weight problem in their lives. My initial reaction, and response to these weight loss companies: SERIOUSLY? Way to go weight loss industry. Way to make us feel better about ourselves. Way to sabotage our efforts before we've ever even started. This problem is not just in weight loss companies. This permeates our media, throughout the world. A recent magazine cover in Europe, featuring Adele, British singer and beautiful plus sized woman, drew controversy. The magazine chose to focus on her face, not showing Adele as she is, beautiful, curves and all. We need to face the facts. Those of us who were not made thin aren't going to be thin. But we can be thinner, lose weight, to feel better in our own skin, to have more energy, to be healthy, help us feel better about ourselves, and countless other reasons. Isn't that what weight loss is supposed to be about?

For those that chose not to see women for who and what they are, beautiful creatures that were designed to have curves, I have news for you...Fat women exist. We have curves. We are beautiful. We are sexy. We are worthy of love. This year I'm going to try and lose weight. Not for a man, not to prove any statistics...FOR ME.

I exist. I have curves. I am beautiful. I am sexy. Regardless of my shape or size, I am worthy of love.

Changes 01/05/2012

I don't like change. Well, let me clarify-I don't like all change.

Times change. Seasons change. Feelings change. Thoughts change. Plans change. The world changes. People change.

I don't mind positive changes. Changes that are good can bring marvelous things. But not all changes are marvelous.

It seems that we are in a symbiotic relationship with change. When change happens, it is not an occurrence all to itself.

There is always an effect that follows change. A begets B.
One thing cannot change without causing change to another.

Think about it. If you're in a bad mood, and your best friend tells you to smile, you're going to smile.

If you and your significant other have a fight, and words are exchanged, words you wish you could take back, both parties are forever changed.

I've heard it said that we should "embrace change." A good friend told me once that everything changes, and that we should enjoy it.

I don't feel the same way. At least with all changes. Good changes, positive changes, are fine with me.

It's the negative changes, or the changes that happen to me, not for me, the changes that are beyond my control are the ones
I have a harder time with.

Postcard from the Moon   01/22/2012

Hello. I thought I'd take a moment to write you.

I have arrived on the moon safe and sound.

I came here with my great friend S.

While here I have made another friend, J.

I have even met a mime and a Pierrot while here on the moon, believe it or not.

My work here has been very detailed and meticulous in nature.

It's been very tedious at times.

That being said, it's also been very challenging and exciting.

I think I'll be here for a little while longer-another few months at least.

But don't worry, I am not alone. My friends S, J, Mime and Pierrot are with me.

You should see the Earth from here-it's beautiful.
It looks so calm, so peaceful. Our home is so beautiful.

You should also see what's here, besides the footprints in the surface.

You never know what you'll find, in the moon. I should draw this letter to a close. I'll be home soon.

When you miss me, look at the moon and think of me.

I'm never far.

A Magical Night   1/26/2012

I remember I was so excited when I heard that he was going to come to my town. Marcel Marceau, here, in person. I was so excited to hear that he was coming.

He had given a performance in another town in my state several years before. But now, finally he was coming to my town.

I finally held the Holy Grail in my hands, the ticket to his show.

I remember when the night came I was ecstatic. The theater was alive with energy as we the audience sat there, waiting for the magic to begin.

It would soon become clear that this was no ordinary night at the theater. A night of fantasy, magic and enchantment awaited us.

The lights finally went down. I had waited for this moment my whole life. The curtain opened and the lights came on. The master himself came onto the stage.

There, on the stage, was Marcel Marceau, the greatest mime in the world. The audience rose and cheered and applauded. The sound was deafening. We stood and applauded for minutes on end.

The applause finally died down. The show began.

I remember sitting there, enraptured. Monsieur Marceau had the entire theater in the palm of his hand.

Over the course of the evening he had the audience laughing in hysterics and weeping from emotion.

Regrettably, as the years have passed, I have lost certain details in my memory about that night. However, there are moments about that night that I will never forget.

I remember sitting there spellbound, transported to another place in time, in rapt attention, completely enchanted.

I never had the good fortune to meet Monsieur Marceau, and I would only see him on the stage this one time.

I am not a mime, and have never studied it. But that evening made an impression on me that will last a lifetime.

In a time before cell phones, computers and the internet, Monsieur Marceau was known the world over. He was and still is an iconic figure throughout the world.

After his passing in 2007, the world mourned his passing, as did I.

I am one of a precious few of many thousands of people around the world who are privileged to say that they saw him perform live.

Marcel Marceau will always be remembered for showing us ourselves, the world around us, our humanity, and inhumanity.

I am Hope

I'm Home   02/15/2012

I've made my voyage and am home from the moon.

I have learned many things while I was gone. I've learned that people have many sides, like those of the moon. Someone can tell you they're one thing, when they're really the opposite.

I have learned that I have to protect myself and guard what I hold dear.

I learned that my best friends will always be on my side, no matter what.

I have learned that I have friends that care about me and love me. I learned my friends only want the best for me.

I will be making a return voyage to the Moon very shortly. While there I will learn many new things I'm sure.

Each voyage is a new adventure, a new opportunity to learn new things, about myself, my friends, the world, the moon.

On every voyage, I am never alone. My dear friends are with me. The true voyage is theirs, not mine.

But I have to say, the adventure is so fulfilling. I'm grateful to have been asked along for the ride.

Now that I have been to the moon, I have a new passion, a new affinity for it. It will always hold a special place in my heart.

And I will return to the moon again.

But for now…
       …I'm home.

Milestones   02/22/2012

I recently had a milestone-the anniversary of the date of my adoption. I am about to have another milestone-a milestone birthday. I want to take a moment to thank everyone who has helped me along the way. You've helped me become the person I am today. I want to thank the universe for finding me the right family. I feel like I am where I need to be. I want to thank my friends, my best friends: A, L, A, B, R, M, G, P, S, X, and Sally. Your friendship means more to me than you can know. Thank you also to the friends who aren't currently in my life. I learned something from each and every one of you. As I travel the road ahead I know there are many more milestones to come.
I can't wait to meet all of them.

Writer's Block   03/01/2012

I can't do this. I was sitting here, writing a poem, wanting to express what I feel, what I want, what is in my heart. But I can't. I'm blocked. The words are like fireflies flying above my head. They are elusive and won't let me catch them, or even admire their beauty. It is so frustrating to want to say something, but not have the wherewithal to say it. You know you want to say something, that you have to say something, but it just won't come out. The words won't come to you, for whatever reason. When the words and thoughts align, the result is a piece of art, something truly magical. But when they don't, when you can't even put a sentence together to express yourself, when the words are elusive and can't be found, when inspiration won't come, when frustration and doubt enter the picture, it can be a horrible feeling. I saw a quote once: "Even if it's crap, get it on the page." Easier said than done.

Lies 03/08/2012

Last night a new acquaintance of mine lied to me. To my face. I asked him a question, he lied to my face. This person is no longer my acquaintance.

This person and I didn't know each other very well, and we only knew each other for a few months. But his intentionally lying to me is something I can't tolerate.

Lies come in different forms and even colors. Where I live we have "little white lies," little lies that are seen as inconsequential and do no harm. For example:

"No honey, you don't look fat in that dress, you look beautiful."

"No, I wouldn't like to sign up for one of your store's credit cards to save 5%-I already have one."

"No, I liked the movie. That one actor was brilliant."

"Let's do this again sometime."

Again, these little white lies are to spare a person's feelings, and aren't intended to do harm. But then there are lies that have an effect on other people's lives. Things that people should say to one another, things people should know, things that will hurt deeply once the truth is told, things that could change a person's life.

Those are the lies that hurt the most, and must be told. It will hurt the other person without a doubt. But the person would much rather be told the truth:

"I'm gay." "I'm in love with someone else." "I don't love you the way you love me." "I'm engaged to be married and I'm going to have a baby." Those are examples of things that need to be said.

These lies don't have a name. Perhaps they should be called "big black lies."

A friend told me that "everyone lies." I won't deny that-I have lied. My lies are in the "little white lie" category. I have never lied about anything that would change a person's life. But I have certainly been on the receiving end of lies from the other category.

If I had been better friends with this person, been more emotionally invested, I would have gone to them again and ask why they lied to me.

But since this person and I weren't very close, I decided to let the acquaintance out of my life. I don't need dishonesty.

When a person lies to another person, in the "big black lies" category, they're basically saying, "I don't care about you enough to tell you the truth."

If you have something to tell someone, something you've been lying about, come clean.

The truth will hurt, but the person will know that you are finally being honest.

Learn about trust and forgiveness, on both sides. Care enough about the other person to finally tell them the truth.

I am Hope

Dear Moon   03/11/2012

Luna, my moon, dear friend, thank you for coming to my window last night.

I went to bed and quickly noticed that there was an abundance of light in the room….your light.

I looked out the window, and there you were, right outside my window, shining just for me.

You brought me so much comfort last night, Luna.

Just knowing you were there filled me with hope.

I looked at you and felt so much warmth in my soul.

I knew that, whatever happens, everything's going to be alright.

Thank you for coming to me last night, Luna.

Your being there was exactly what I needed.

Thank you, dear friend.

See you tonight.

Let the Magic Begin 03/15/2012

I've been thinking about the concept of change. As I have said before, I am not a fan of change. Change can leave me feeling uncomfortable, insecure about things. The thought that I have to change, in order to get the things that I want, to make my dreams come true, does not leave a pleasant taste in my mouth.

But then I heard three words that changed my view of the word change, or, the changes that I must undergo. The first word is "evolve." The word has a positive connotation to it, is without stigmas or Pavlovian reflexes. In thinking about the words, I would much rather evolve as a person than change.

Another word is "renaissance." This is a word full of hope, also with positive connotations, and shows the depth and complexities involved.

The third word that I found was "transform." That also evokes positive images, and is a more preferable word than change.

I have likened my progression as a person and writer in the last two years as a "metamorphosis." I like that word as well.

Evolve-Renaissance-Transformation-Metamorphosis.

Those are words that reflect the differences in me that must occur if my dreams are to come true. With those words in mind, I embrace the differences to come, not the changes.

The evolution. The renaissance. The transformation. The metamorphosis. A wondrous, magical process.

Let the magic begin.

Daydreams   03/16/2012

Dreams are something that usually come to us as we're sleeping at night.

However, I have to tell you, my most fulfilling experience with dreams have been while I've been wide awake.

I prefer to dream while awake, because I get to choose what I dream. If I don't like how the dream is going, I can change it.

Lately I've been dreaming of a new life.

Quitting my job, maybe living in a new city, maybe in a new country, making a living as writer, being creative and being paid for it.

Each time I daydream the subject changes.

The wealth of possibilities, as are things to dream about, are endless.

I don't know if my dreams will come true or not.

I tell you, I'm having so much fun dreaming about things, the way they can be.

You should see what I see.

My life is going to be so beautiful.

Many have heard Shakespearean quote "to sleep perchance to dream."

I have changed the quote as it pertains to me:

"To wake perchance to dream."

My Indigo Knight 03/19/2012

I have been thinking about the qualities I would like to have in the man of my dreams, should he ever come. I'm not looking for Prince Charming, a white knight, a knight in shining armor. I'm saving my love for an indigo knight.

Here are some of the qualities he will possess. He must:

- be passionate about his work
- be non-materialistic
- be employed
- be funny
- be talented
- be caring and compassionate
- be more fascinated in me than he is in himself
- treat me like a queen
- care about what I'm thinking and feeling
- be supportive of the things I want
- be open and honest
- love cats
- love when I sing
- pass the friends and family test
- be my #1 fan
- be my best friend
- be indigo
- recognize the beauty in a smile
- see the beauty in me
- love what he sees when he looks at me
- love me

A Year Later   03/28/2012

Last year, I had been writing poems off and on, and sharing them with some of my friends. They loved my poetry and encouraged me to write more.

Then I had the idea, "Why not create a blog? My friend has a blog; maybe I could have one too." I then went to that friend and asked him what he thought.

He loved the idea. He said that I deserved my own blog. He was right.

I began this blog a year ago today.

At first, I only had the blog as a private blog; I was still insecure about my writing, so I only had the blog available to my closest friends.

But as I built the blog site I began to build my character of Esperanza Habla. (No, that is not my God given name.)

But in creating this character, and in writing poetry for this blog, it has opened the world to me.

I began this blog with the poem "Thank Yous." I echo those thanks today. Those friendships initiated my journey to the moon and back, which changed my life forever.

To date there have been over 3,500 visits to this blog, from the United States, Peru, Germany, Russia, Spain, Luxembourg, Colombia, Mexico, Ukraine, the United Kingdom, Canada, Portugal, Chile, Venezuela, Puerto Rico, Italy, the Dominican Republic, Costa Rica, France, and more.

When I began writing poetry, I just did it to express what I was thinking and feeling.

I never dreamed that I'd have a worldwide audience, reading my words, thoughts, feelings, reading me-and coming back to read what I have to say.

I cannot thank you enough for reading what I write and coming back to read more. Thank you for listening, for reading, for caring about what I have to say.

As I have progressed as a poet I have also begun a business translating written works for authors from Spanish into English.

I have translated three books to date. I've even transferred this skill into translating movies.

I have also begun to write my first novel, called "Samantha." I want to take a moment to personally thank my family and friends for their support of this literary endeavor. Your support means more to me than you can ever know.

Thank you to my dear friend S, for your support and creative partnership, and for teaching me how to fly.

Thank you to my dear friend Sally, to whom this blog is dedicated. I love you and I miss you. Rest in peace, dear friend.

And to you, my readers. I cannot thank you enough for reading my poetry and coming back to read more. Thank you for listening, for reading, for caring about what I have to say.

The world is truly an amazing place. Now that I have found my path, my life will never be the same.

I am Hope

Dear Sally   03/30/2012

Dear Sally, we lost you a year ago. A year ago today. I can't believe you're gone. I remember that night, the night you died, I talked to you. Thank you for having God send me the feeling of warmth and comfort I needed so badly. I've not talked to you very much since then. It's not because I didn't want to-I don't want to hold you back-I want your spirit to be free, to fly wherever you want, wherever your spirit takes you.

S is fine-of course, you know this already. I remember that he went to the moon to visit you. Thank you for being such a welcoming host. He really needed to get away from it all for a while. Thank you for being there for him. The book is coming along-we hope to publish it this year. Have you read it already? If not, you're going to love it. Thank you so much for helping him write it. It's a story of such sweetness, tenderness, warmth, love, the important things in life.

It would seem that today would not be the right day to celebrate your life, on the day that you left us. But today I celebrate you. I celebrate your life and the friendship we shared. I celebrate the lunches we spent together, the laughs we shared, your compassion, the lives you touched.

I miss writing you every week, sending you cards, letting you know what was going on in my life, with my poetry, with my new friends. Since you've gone, I find I'm not sending many cards anymore. I still remember the last one I sent you......
"Sally, in case I never told you, I am a different person for having known you. Thank you for our many years of laughter, fun and friendship. I love you, my forever Sally-Pooh."

Thank you for coming for a visit, so I could talk to you again. You will forever be my shining light. I love you and I miss you, my forever Sally-Pooh...

The Milestone Birthday   04/17/2012

Last week I had a milestone birthday. As the day approached over the last months, I had visions of spending my birthday in Las Vegas, or Lima, Peru, Paris, or some other exotic faraway place. My travel plans weren't meant to be. I was meant to be just where I am. It wasn't what I thought it was going to be; in many ways, it was better. I received the gifts of a new kitchen appliance, a few cards, a night out at the movies, my first interview, a poem written just for me, many well wishes on Facebook, a book about a man In the Moon, and many blessings of family and friends. The best part about this birthday was spending it with my parents; my mother had a milestone birthday as well. My parents and I took a day to escape our cities and travel to a nearby hamlet, less than an hour drive away. We had a great lunch, and then went to an amazing museum and art gallery. The artist had pieces for sale, and I bought two of them as a birthday gift for myself. After our shopping, we went to a nearby café. We each ordered one dessert. Our desserts arrived, but not our drinks yet. So, we toasted one another with our forks. We held them up, toasted my mother's birthday, then mine, and then clinked forks. The desserts and the day in the hamlet were delicious. Afterwards we came back to my place, so I could give my mother her gift-an mp3 player. She didn't expect it, and absolutely loved it. I'd been planning giving her the music player for months, but was unsure of her reaction to receiving a piece of technology as a birthday present. To my delight, she loves the mp3 player. I had pre-loaded the player with music that I thought she would like. I think she's used it just about every day since I gave it to her. I also gave her cords and cables and gadgets to help make the mp3 player more user-friendly. I know that it will be a gift that she will love and use for years to come. And that makes my heart happy. My mother was overwhelmed with her gifts. I then told her, "Well, you'll only have this milestone birthday once, just like me." I thank everyone for all of their gifts, cards, messages of love and well wishes on my special day. It was truly a milestone birthday.

Life   4/27/2012

I've heard it said that life is many things-a journey, a highway, a dream, a gift, a banquet, a puzzle, a gamble, a story, a movie, a song, a cabaret, an adventure, a cereal, a board game.

I've been thinking about my life, the way things are now, the way they've been, the way I want them to be.

My life as it is now is not as I want it. That being said, there is plenty of room for growth, potential and time to achieve the things I want out of life.

To me, life isn't any of these things. Like the best of all things, life, to me, is a verb.

What I Want Out of Life   05/01/2012

What do I want out of life? I want to be a successful writer.
I want for my writing to be a lucrative endeavor. I want to have a life in the arts. I want to continue my creative collaboration.
I want to help others by translating their written works.
I want to live the life that I want, the life that I deserve.

I also want simple things. I want to share my life with someone. I want to find love. I want to love. I want to be loved. I want to marry. I want to know that I am married to my best friend.
I want to be blissfully, completely, sickeningly happy.

Not a long list, but a sincere one.

Greater Than, Less Than, Equal To   05/06/2012

For anyone who has had to suffer through classes in math, there are concepts known as "greater than", "less than" and "equal to."

I was never any good at math, as any of my family members can tell you. But, in my meager understanding, as an example, 3 is greater than 2, 3 is less than 5, and 3 is equal to 3. I think I have the basics of it.

However, one of these concepts has seeped out of the math books and into our lives-"less than." This concept has permeated our lives.

If a woman has to lose a breast to cancer, she might think of herself as "less of a woman." If a man is considering a vasectomy, he might think himself "less than a man."

But this concept is not just an individual phenomenon-it is a societal one as well. If a man chooses to live his life alone, he is seen as an "eligible bachelor." If a woman chooses to live alone, or chooses not to have children, or has no love currently in her life, she is looked upon with pity. Like something is wrong with her. Like she is less of a woman.

These views are ludicrous. Why should a man's choice to remain single be seen as "greater than" a woman who chooses the same thing? Why should a woman be seen as "less than" in the same circumstances?

This is not a trend that is only seen in my country, it is a global phenomenon. If I choose to live life alone, that is my choice. If I never find love, so be it. I will never have children, and don't want them. But those are my choices, and the choices I will make. It doesn't mean I'm less of a woman. It doesn't mean my choices are greater than yours.

The choices you've made in your life, up to this point, have brought you to the place you are in life.

It doesn't matter if you're in a committed relationship, married, single, in a domestic partnership, sharing your life with someone without being married, choosing to live life alone, a parent to a child or a parent to a pet.

We've all made choices in our lives, and we have to live with our choices. But the choices we make should not be compared to those of others, and should not be judged by society.

Our choices, our lives are not "greater than" or "less than." They are equal to.

"Equal To" by Esperanza Habla

Gone Too Soon 05/21/2012

I have noticed recently-maybe you have as well, that the world has lost many famous people this year, including Whitney Houston, Dick Clark, Donna Summer, Etta James, Maurice Sendak, Davy Jones and Robin Gibb. They join the ranks of those who have gone too soon-James Dean, Marilyn Monroe, Karen Carpenter, Buddy Holly, Natalie Wood, and countless others.

It is an interesting phenomenon to me when a celebrity dies. The reaction to hearing of their death can range from a "who?" to "I thought they were already dead," to "What?!?!?!?" to an "awwwwww." The news can have little to no effect on us, or can sadden us deeply and affect us for days.

It seems to me that, the more upset we are about a celebrity death, the more we were affected by that person. We valued what they did, their art, and their contribution to the world. It also means that that person had an effect on our lives. A genuine effect. When you know all the words to their songs, or can recite the lines they said in a movie, can picture the drawings in their books, the images in their music videos, this is a genuine effect.

When a famous person dies, it can feel like a friend, or loved one has died, even though we never met them. Celebrate these artists. Sing their songs. Watch their movies. Read their books. Time is their eternal friend. Through their chosen mediums, they will live forever.

I leave you with a song the Bee Gees wrote about the loss of their brother Andy. They wrote it for him-it's now for Andy Gibb, Maurice Gibb, Robin Gibb, and all those who have gone too soon.

Poet of the Moon   05/25/2012

An intriguing concept, to be a poet of the moon. That seems to be me. I seem to be the poet of the moon. I have been called "Dame of the Moon." "Princess of the Moon." "Poetess of the Moon." "Moon Woman." I am of the moon. It is hard to describe the influence the moon has had on my life. It has magnified friendships. It has helped me learn to fly. It has come to my aid in times of strife. It has welcomed me with open arms. It has sheltered me and brought me comfort. It has transported me to its surface and beyond, in ways I never could have imagined. I am of the moon. You can call me whatever you want. Poet of the moon is fine with me.

Mirrors   05/25/2012

Funny things mirrors. On first glance, they show a reflection. But is that really all that we see? In literature and folklore, mirrors have transported Alice into Wonderland, shown us our innermost desires, even hidden evil spirits behind them. I am not interested in the mirrors themselves, but in their reflections. For me, when I look into a mirror, that is just a reflection. That is a reflection of my body, of my face. Not my soul. That's just my body-it's not me. I cannot see myself in a mirror. My soul, my spirit, cannot be seen. I am more than I can see in the mirror. I believe the reflection we see of ourselves in the mirror is the reflection we believe we can see.

"Study me as much as you like, you will never know me, for I differ a hundred ways from what you see me to be. Put yourself behind my eyes, and see me as I see myself, for I have chosen to dwell in a place you cannot see."—Rumi

I am Hope

The Keeper of the Key   06/12/2012

It seems to me, in matters of the heart, as it is said, the course of true love never did run smooth. I have also heard that there is a lid for every pot, a person for every person on the planet. Someone special destined just for us to love.

I have seen types of parties for single people where keys and locks are exchanged-women receive locks on a necklace, men likewise receive keys. The point is to mingle around the party, talk to different people, and find out which gentleman has the key to fit your lock. It's a clever idea for such an event, and a neat ice breaker, to meet people.

But in life, in reality, I don't think it works that way. For me, or for any of us.

There is a wall around my heart. Beyond that there is a lock, and there is a key. But no man has the key to my heart. I have the key.

I am the guardian of the wall around my heart. I keep guard over the lock.

And when I find him, my indigo knight, the man who
I am destined to spend the rest of my life with, I will decide when and if to give him the key.

No man can come with a key looking to see if it fits the lock in my heart.

I will decide who to give the key to and when. I will do so when I am ready.

That is how it has to be, for I am the keeper of the key.

When My Cat Howls   06/14/2012

I hate when my cat howls. It's disturbing. Unnerving. She's beginning to do it daily, several times. Every time she does it her howling comes out of nowhere. The sounds that come out of her are ungodly, unearthly. It sounds like she's in terrible pain, or if her fur were on fire. Such intense, guttural howling from this cat. She does it all hours of the day. And night. At 5 in the morning it's particularly terrifying. I've asked my sister about it (my sister knows more about cats than I do). She said that the howling is a sign of senility. The cat's grasping with a bombardment of sights and sounds that they don't understand. So, to comfort themselves, they just sit and howl. That makes sense. My cat is seventeen years old, has lost most of her hearing, and is probably going senile.
It makes sense. But I hate it. I was in my office working the other day when I heard the loudest, ungodly sound come out of her. It was a howl I'd never heard before. I ran in the other room to check on her. There she was, looking at me, as if to say, "What????"

I hate when my cat howls.

"Calypso the Cat" by Esperanza Habla

The Death of a Friendship   06/20/2012

The death of a friendship can be a terrible thing. Sometimes a friendship fades over time. Sometimes a friendship fades away due to a move in location. Sometimes a friendship dies because the friends grow apart and someone wants out. Whatever the reason, the death of a friendship can be a painful thing.

I have recently experienced the death of a friendship. I spoke to a friend about it, to get some counsel. Her words to me were: "It stinks, it sucks, and you are not alone." It is nice to know that this person understands what I'm going through. I know I'm not alone.

I learned many life lessons from the friendship that died. I even learned a new language. I am grateful for everything that I have learned.

I want to thank my family and my dear friends for their unending support.

About the Author

Esperanza Habla is the pen name of the indigo Poet of the Moon. She began her writing career in 2010, launching her first blog, **"Words of Hope"**, with poetry written in English and Spanish. In 2012 she created another blog, **"Letters to the Moon."** Both blogs have acquired a growing readership made up of readers in over 40 countries around the world. In 2013 Esperanza established her own publishing company, **La Luna Press, L.L.C.**

Esperanza holds a Bachelor's Degree from Marian College in Music History and Literature. Having a musical background, she loves to watch movies, attend theater productions, musical performances and poetry readings. Her work as a poet and artist has garnered her a place in a worldwide collective community of creative artists. She loves to support other artists as she herself has been helped. She has been featured as the Author of the Day and her written work has won Honorable Mention in literary contests.

Esperanza lives in the United States and shares her life with her dear family and two kittens. She can be found on her website:

www.esperanzahabla.com

www.ingramcontent.com/pod-product-compliance
Lightning Source LLC
Chambersburg PA
CBHW041403090426
42743CB00006B/138